Long Island's Religious History

Compiled by

JANE des GRANGE

Director, Suffolk Museum

Distributed by

IRA J. FRIEDMAN, INC.

Port Washington, N. Y.

Suffolk Museum

Stony Brook, L.I., New York

"The stranger who sojourns with you shall be to you as the native among you, and you shall love him as yourself . . ."

Leviticus, 19:34

"If well executed, a history of Long Island, with special reference to its moral and religious conditions, cannot fail to be deeply instructive to the present inhabitants and their numerous kindred, scattered as they are in every part of this wide-spread land.

The tide of emigration has been greater than is imagined - you will find natives of the Island in all quarters of the land the clannish feeling probably exists in greater strength in no part of our country, than among the natives and descendants of Suffolk County.

Nor is it to the natives of the Island or their descendants alone, that such a history will be interesting and instructive. It is a part of the country, which, till within a few years, was scarcely known to non-residents. It was so far removed - so difficult of access, and presented so few inducements to wander through its forests, and wander through its sands, that for the space of 200 years it has remained, in a great measure, terra incognita, to almost the whole world. It is true, that most people have learned from their geography and maps, that there is such an island, stretching along the broad Atlantic, defending the city of New York and the whole shore of Connecticut from the fury of the ocean waves; and they have heard a thousand exaggerated stories of the ignorance and simplicity of the inhabitants. And it must be confessed, that the insular situation and other physical obstacles, have necessarily operated to limit the views and retard the progress of the mind, when confined to such narrow boundaries. In this respect it is true, that in the views of the islanders generally, the affairs of this wide world are drawn on a somewhat contracted scale.

And it is equally true, that from their non-intercourse with the cunning and dishonest men of the world, (for be it known, that a consummate rogue is about as rare an animal as a wolf on Long Island), they are an unsuspecting people, and are perhaps more easily over-reached than those who are more conversant with the ways of the world. But for good common sense, sound judgment, and general information, so far as it may be obtained from books and oral instruction, they are not inferior to the mass of population, in any equal portion of the state."

From "History of Long Island" by Nathaniel S. Prime, 1845

This was written nearly one hundred and twenty years ago, but the words seem timeless, as did Pope John's when he said:

"Every man has the right to honor God according to the dictates of an upright conscience."

It is my hope that these monographs and the exhibition of ecclesiastical art that accompany their publication, will help you to 'sojourn' a little better with your fellow man - will help you to understand the religious heritage that is his.

December 1, 1963

Jane des Grange, Director

Genesis

Just as Long Island was first settled by the English and Dutch, two nationalities differing in language but akin in a common devotion to political freedom, so the first churches, the Puritan and the Dutch Reformed, though differing in language and customs, had a common heritage in an evangelical faith strongly rooted in the community.

Long Island at its western extremity was separated from the Little Dutch settlement of Nieuw Amsterdam by the East River, and the eastern forks were readily accessible to the English settlements in Massachusetts and Connecticut. It was natural, therefore, that colonists from Nieuw Amsterdam and New England should make the comparatively easy journey to this island abounding in shell fisheries and fertile farm land at its two extremities.

In the case of the English, the initial settlements were church centered communities - little Zions in a strange land centered about that cradle of American liberty in things religious, educational and political, the "meeting house."

In the summer of 1640 the first two churches were established, one at Southold and the other at Southampton. These puritan theocracies on the eastern end of Long Island are represented today by their descendants in the Presbyterian and Congregational denominations.

Further to the west within the boundary of the Dutch jurisdiction, English churches had also been organized. Governors Kieft and Stuyvesant who fiercely opposed the intrusion of Quakers, Roman Catholics, Jews, Lutherans and Anglicans, welcomed English Presbyterians as fellow Calvinists.

The other great settlements and churches were, as we have noted, the Dutch. While not fired with the puritan fervor to build little Zions in a brave new world, the sober Dutch attracted by the prospects of ample farms and fisheries and the burgeoning fur trade, built their houses of worship - often small but neat hexagonal structures and gathered for worship "of Zondag". One of the principal problems was a shortage of trained ministers and while the Classis of Amsterdam attempted to supply the infant settlements it was difficult to secure trained men who would make the long journey and settle far from their familiar associations in these primitive colonies.

Nieuw Amsterdam had been early supplied with ministers; first, Jonas Michaelius, then the doughty Everadus Bogardus, and Fort Orange (Albany) with the learned and kindly Johannes Megapolensis, but the hamlets at the western end of Long Island - Brueckelen, Midwout (Flatbush) and Nieuw Amersfoort (Flatlands) and the still smaller settlements of Boswyck (Bushwick), Nieuw Utrecht, Gravesend (in what is now Kings County) and Flushing, Rusdorp, and Newtown, in what is now Queens and Hempstead in the present Nassau County, lacked "dominies" of the Dutch church. Gravesend, Rusdorp (Jamaica), Newtown and Hempstead were largely English in population and posed little problem as they generally supplied their own ministers.

English settlers led by Lady Deborah Moody and Nicholas Stilwell formed the core of the Dutch Reformed Church at Gravesend (1655). The larger settlements in the modern Brooklyn caused Governor Stuyvesant, a loyal son of the Reformed Church, much concern. He had brought as a temporary supply preacher, the Rev. Johannes Backerus, from Curacao, who had been succeeded by the able Megapolensis who had resigned his post in Albany and had intended to return to Holland. The ubiquitous and multilingual Samuel Drisius had been sent to assist in the outlying areas and was soon busy assisting in the towns and the settlements in New Jersey and Staten Island among the Huguenots, English and Dutch settlers.

In 1653 a momentous arrival marked a great change in the religious history of the area when the "St. Charles", a vessel from Pernambuco (Recife), Brazil, anchored off the battery with a group of exiles from that colony which had recently come under Portuguese rule. Stuyvesant balked at admitting the Jewish passengers, but welcomed the well trained and able Johannes Theodorus Polhemus who was quickly assigned to the hamlets across the East River. Early in 1654, the energetic Polhemus organized churches in Brooklyn, Flatbush, and Flatlands - all of which are still flourishing. According to tradition, Polhemus crossed over in the ferry with his horse and saddlebags and organized all three churches on the same day.

While the priority of the first church is a matter of dispute, it is only a matter of hours! In the following year the Gravesend Church was organized and in 1661 the church at Bushwick, where the French-speaking Drisius was officiating. The last Dutch Church to be organized in Brooklyn in the colonial period was the Nieuw Utrecht congregation organized in 1677 under Dominie van Zuuren.

Denominations, other than Presbyterian and Congregational, were comparatively late on Long Island. Even after the English conquest of the Dutch in 1664, it was 34 years before Trinity Church was founded in New York (1698).

The Dutch predominated in Brooklyn for a century and a quarter. Dominie Martinus Schoonmaker who died 1824, and his brother Henricus, were among the last Dutch preachers in the older churches.

In 1794 Bishop Asbury of the Methodist Church notes that "I went over to Brooklyn where we have a small society. I had very few hearers except those who came from the city. I administered the sacrament and we had some life." Thereafter Methodism grew apace.

The Baptists had congregations here in the 1800's, the Unitarians in 1833, and the Lutherans began to appear in the 1840's and '50's. The first Congregational Church was organized in the 1840's. Roman Catholics had to go, by boat, to mass in New York until the first parish was established in the 1820's, the third in Sag Harbor. The Bowne House in Flushing housed the first Quaker Meeting in 1636.

The attempt of Stuyvesant to suppress the Quakers in 1657 elicited two classic statements on religious liberty, the famous Remonstrance signed by 30 citizens of the community, and the directive of the West India Company. It is the glory of Flushing that despite the harsh reprisals of the bigoted Stuyvesant, the burghers stood firm and were vindicated by the West India Company and the Estates General.

The Jewish Community in Manhattan dated back to the arrival of the "St. Charles" and its exiles from Brazil including the Dutch Dominie Polhemus in 1654, but there were no organized congregations on Long Island until the middle of the 19th century.

Time fails to record in detail the beginning of many other religious bodies. Three Protestant denominations organized congregations in Brooklyn in the 19th century - the Universalists (1845), the Moravians (1854) and the Swedenborgians (1854). The African Methodist Episcopal Church was or-

3

ganized in 1818 in Brooklyn.
On the Island there are also Eastern
Orthodox Churches - Greek and Russian. Most interestingly what is perhaps the oldest
Christian church in the world, the Syrian Antiochene Orthodox Church, has its Ameri-
can cathedral, St. Nicholas, in Brooklyn, located in the old St. Peters Episcopal
Church on State Street and consecrated in 1902. The only Armenian Orthodox Church
has been dissolved. There are two Polish National Catholic Churches, one in South
Brooklyn and one in Greenpoint. Even the Mohammedans are represented by a center
on State Street and a mosque in Williamsburg.
Truly, Long Island may well be termed

"The Island of Churches."

David Munroe Cory, Th.D., Pastor
Homecrest Presbyterian Church, Brooklyn, N.Y.

African Methodist Episcopal

is an enthusiastic and dedicated Christian movement on Long Island. Typical churches in Setauket, Huntington, Port Washington, Freeport and Amityville originated as small prayerful gatherings which gradually transformed themselves into organized, incorporated churches.

At first, material blessings were scarce. Meager congregations were addressed by travelling preachers who sometimes received no salary. But as the faith took hold, congregations expanded, buildings were erected and preachers became permanent.

The A.M.E. Church and the U.S. Constitution both came into existence in Philadelphia in the year 1789. The Church founder, Richard Allen, a former slave who had purchased his freedom, became a member of the St. George Methodist Episcopal Church in Philadelphia and was given a license to preach. Five years later Allen, ejected from the church by his white brothers, founded his own church in a blacksmith shop. There he and other freed slaves could worship freely.

The African Methodist Episcopal Church, from its humble beginning, grew into a world movement encompassing the United States, Canada, the West Indies, Cuba and Africa.

Many of the early Methodist, Presbyterian, Congregational and Dutch Reformed churches had racially integrated congregations.

In Brooklyn there was an early African Methodist Church the records show, in 1818, a split from the Sand Street Church and the Fleet Street Memorial. In Suffolk County, the Setauket Bethel A.M.E. appears to date from 1815, although the present site was not acquired until 1874.

The Bethel A.M.E. Church in Amityville was founded by Elias Hunter and his wife in 1839. A Sunday School was held in 1841 in the house of David Squires, a house which stands today, on Albany Avenue.

The Bethel A.M.E. Church in Huntington was incorporated in 1843. In the mid 19th Century, the A.M.E. Zion Church and the Ralph Avenue Church were founded in Brooklyn.

From Prime's "History of Long Island" (1845), the following excerpts are taken:

The A.M.E. Church Societies	Members	A.M.E. (Zion) Church Societies	Members
Brooklyn	209	Williamsburgh	34
Flatbush	34	Train's Meadow	20
Jamaica	26	Flushing	59
Flushing	69	Lakeville	78
Cedar Swamp	70	Oysterbay	46
Jericho	15	Jerusalem	47
Huntington	52	Stony Brook	7
So. Huntington	52	Islip and Smithtown	25
Setauket	26	Moriches and Mastick	21
Total	553	Sag Harbour	50
		Total	387

5

He concludes with:

> "There are now over 8,000 negroes on Long Island. The 'African
> Methodist Episcopal Church,' appear to be laudably engaged in
> promoting the interests of their people. They publish a peri-
> odical in New York, which is sustained entirely by contributions
> from their own members; and many of the articles are very re-
> spectable. They have recently held a Convention in Philadelphia,
> at which they resolved to establish a literary institution for
> ministerial education, as soon as funds can be obtained. Such
> praiseworthy efforts deserve encouragement, and substantial aid."

The growing prosperity of Long
Island has been reflected in increased prosperity of the A.M.E. Church. Mortgages
have been burned, organs purchased, and new buildings constructed. Reverend De
Shields, who in 1905 bicycled from Wantagh to Freeport to preach to a congregation
of eight, could drive to church and address a full house today.

William H. Howard from records
collected by Joseph McKenzie, Pastor
Bethel A.M.E. Church, Setauket

St. John's Episcopal, Cold Spring Harbor, 1837

Baptist

In Prime's "History of Long Island"
the following statistics on the Baptist Church appear (1845):

Congregations		Ministers	Membs.
First Church, Brooklyn,		James L. Hodge,	650
Pierpont street,	"	E. E. L. Taylor,	350
South,	"	Vacant,	70
Williamsburgh,	"	Alanson P. Mason,	160
Newtown,		Vacant,	21
Oysterbay,		Marmaduke Earle,	60
Cold Spring,		--------- Earle,	
Coram,		Vacant,	28
Greenport,		Alvin Ackley,	151
Sag Harbour,			93
Total,	10	 6	1583

In Oyster Bay, "the first recorded religious organization is of the Baptist persua-
sion. Only a few facts have been gleaned by Marmaduke Earle, the 1845 pastor.

About the year 1700 the preacher Wm.
Rhodes came to us, having a short time before emigrated from England to Rhode Island.
By his labours he collected a small number of hearers. But whether he was ever ordained or a church actually organized under his ministry, does not appear.   About
1724 a house of worship was erected. It is about 20 ft. square, with 12 ft. posts,
and a pyramidal roof running to a sharp point. Though removed to the opposite side of
the street and converted into a barn, with a 'lean-to' on each side, it still continues to attract the notice of every stranger.

The present church edifice was erect-
ed in 1805. In 1724 Robert Feeks was ordained by Elders from Rhode Island and was
called a 'free-will' baptist, and 'as no other qualification was considered necessary
in a candidate for baptism, than a desire to be saved, his church was of course numerous."

In 1747 a Baptist meeting house was
erected in Coram and an early church organized. This was supposed to be the first,
and for a long time, the only one of its kind in the County.

In Brookhaven records, it is noted
that in 1820 Congregationalists, Methodists, Presbyterians and Baptists united to
build a church each using it one-quarter of the time. By 1831 'the last two denominations having run down and the Methodists being in want' .. it was purchased by them.

The Baptist church was the first
erected in Greenport and the building was moved there in 1833. In 1845 there were
151 members. The people in Rocky Point were angry about the removal of their church
and built another, though there was no organization there. A Baptist church was organized in Cold Spring Harbor in 1843; a house of worship was built in 1845. In
1844 there was a church built in Sag Harbor.

A few simple notes compiled from the only
material available to the Museum.   JDG

9

Christian Science

Christian Science was introduced on Long Island in 1892 by Mrs. Sadie Skidmore of Philadlephia. A few friends met in her summer cottage at Port Jefferson. Nine members participated and conducted a Sunday School. When Mrs. Skidmore's small home would no longer accommodate the people attending, a room was secured, first in Athena Hall, later known as Port Jefferson Theater, and then in the Good Templar's Hall. Summer congregations numbered in the 50's.

The group continued holding meetings until 1905. New interest in Christian Science in the Port Jefferson area around 1925 eventually led to the establishment of the present church, First Church of Christ, Scientist, Port Jefferson Station.

Rockville Centre and Southampton were two other Long Island communities in which an early interest developed. The first Rockville Centre services, at which four families were present, were held November 21, 1904, in a private home. The following Wednesday a mid-week meeting was held, and a Sunday School was soon formed. This informal group dissolved in 1908, but a number of the former participants again began holding informal meetings in 1910. This led to the establishment on June 10, 1924, of First Church of Christ, Scientist, Rockville Centre.

Mrs. Anna J. Drew and Mrs. Mary Howell started services in Southampton in 1906. The group continued to grow until it became established at its present site on Cameron and Pine Streets as First Church of Christ, Scientist, Southampton.

Christian Science was introduced in Hempstead in 1909 and in six other Long Island communities, including: Lynbrook(1914), Patchogue (1915), Bay Shore (1915), Northport (1917), Glen Cove (1918) and Huntington (1919).

The first Christian Science lecture was given under the auspices of the Hempstead Society in 1913 by Virgil O. Strickler.

A Christian Science church may not be dedicated until free from debt, its mortgage has been paid off and all indebtedness satisfied.

Today there are 21 of these churches on Long Island and 12 in the Borough of Queens, and six in the Borough of Brooklyn. There are Christian Science organizations at Hofstra College, Hempstead and the United States Merchant Marine Academy, Kings Point, as well as at Queens College, Flushing.

DeWitt John, Mgr. Publications Committee
Mother Church, Boston

11

Congregational

Congregationalism first came to Long
Island in 1640, when Rev. John Youngs and a small group of pioneers settled in Southold but today's congregational churches arose mainly from the "Great Awakening" of
1740. The Strict Congregational Movement in Connecticut resulted when the state-
dominated ecclesiastical organization took the place of the freedom of earlier congregationalism, and the harsh legislation of the Connecticut colonial legislature was
enacted in 1743 for the express purpose of suppressing the Strict Congregationalists.

As a result of the Great Awakening, a
number of churches arose in southeastern Connecticut which had seceded from the "Established Order." At that time the Established Order in Connecticut consisted of the
Congregational and Presbyterian churches - the names being used interchangeably. The
seceding churches were called "Separate" or "New Light" churches. This Separatist
Movement was, to a large degree, a protest against the departure of 18th century congregationalism from its earlier ideals. The Separates preferred to call themselves
"Strict Congregationalists," implying that they alone of the congregational churches
followed the original principles of the founding forefathers who had fled from Scrooby
to settle the Plymouth Colony in 1620.

The physical closeness of Connecticut
to Long Island and the ease of transportation across the Sound firmly implanted the
ideals of the Strict Congregational Movement on Long Island. It also spread to New
Jersey to continue a traceable existence for another 50 years.

All of the oldest of the present Con-
gregational Churches in Suffolk County were founded as "Strict Congregational" churches. The Aquebogue Congregational Church was organized as The First Strict Congregational Church of Southold by Rev. Elisha Paine in 1758. Rev. Paine, of Canterbury,
Conn., is often referred to as the "Moses" of the Strict Congregationalists.

As a result of the open warfare be-
tween the Strict Congregationalists and the Colonial government of Connecticut, Rev.
Paine finally went into voluntary exile and finished his years as pastor of a small
Separate Church in Bridgehampton. It was during this period of exile that he organized the Aquebogue church.

The Wading River Congregational Church
was organized as The Second Strict Congregational Church of Southold in 1787. In
1792, Southold Town was divided into Riverhead and Southold Towns, so that in 1793,
the Third church, organized at Baiting Hollow, was known as The Third Strict Congregational Church of Riverhead.

The Mt. Sinai Congregational Church
was organized in 1789 as The First Strict Congregational Church of Brookhaven. The
Congregational Church of Patchogue was organized as The Second Strict Congregational
Church of Brookhaven in 1793.

Also organized along the same lines
were churches in New Village and Moriches and two Indian churches in Cold Spring and
Poosepatuck.

The Aquebogue church has been referred
to as the "Mother Church" of all the present congregational churches. From this
church was colonized the Orient, Jamesport and Northville (now Sound Avenue) churches.

13

The Northville church further divided to form the Congregational Church of Riverhead. Rev. Noah Hallock of the Mt. Sinai church organized the Patchogue church, which later divided to form the Sayville church.

In addition to these churches and the present Congregational churches in Bayshore, Huntington and Farmingville, there have been Congregational churches in Port Jefferson, Bellport, Greenport, Cutchogue, Commack, South Setauket, Thompson's Station, Fireplace Neck and Blue Point.

In 1791 the Congregational churches and ministers organized themselves into an ecclesiastical association for their mutual benefit, known as The Strict Congregational Convention of Long Island. This organization has continued in existence, under different names, until today, and is the oldest congregational ecclesiastical organization in the state of New York. During its day it has had churches and ministers associated with it in New York, New Jersey and Connecticut. It is known today as The Suffolk County Association of Congregational Churches and Ministers, and continues the original congregational concept of mutual benefit and assistance, while maintaining strict autonomy of individual churches.

Most of the Congregational churches in Suffolk County have voted to combine with the Evangelical and Reformed Churches to form the new United Church of Christ. This union, while it may change the names of some of our Suffolk County Congregationalist Churches in the future, will not affect the traditional independence and autonomy which has always been a characteristic of the Congregationalists.

Jere C. Austin, Historian
Congregationalist Christian Church

Zion Church, Douglaston, 1830

Dutch Reformed, Flatlands
Silver beaker, Boelen, 17th c.
Courtesy Brooklyn Museum

Dutch Reformed

The land on which the present Flatlands Dutch Reformed Church stands, Kings Highway at East 40th Street, was part of the original Andries Huddie-Wolphert Gerritsen purchase from seven Indians in July, 1652.

The section of the borough once known as New Amersfort and later as Flatlands was settled by the Dutch as early as 1636, but no regular services were held until 1654.

There are two church organizations in America that can claim to be older than the Brooklyn Dutch Reformed churches: Marble Collegiate Dutch Reformed in New York City which was originally called the Church in the Fort (1628) and the one founded in Albany in 1632, known as the North Dutch Church.

In 1654 historic records indicate that Peter Stuyvesant, the last of the Dutch governors, at the request of the Long Island Dutch

> "authorized the Rev. Johannes Megapolensis, the Domine of the Church in the Fort, to go across to Long Island and by ecclesiastical authority, to organize a church at New Amersfort, at Midwout (Flatbush) and at Breuckelen."

These were all founded on the same day, February 9, 1654. At first, and for nine years after the church was organized at New Amersfort, religious services were held at the home of Captain Elbert Elbertse Stoothoff.

In 1663 a church was built by the congregation. "It was octagonal, had a belfry and the roof and sides were finished with heavy spruce shingles. It had a wine glass shaped pulpit with a sounding board."

The early congregations were summoned by drumbeat, until in 1686 a bell was imported from the Netherlands and paid for by subscription.

The three churches which were all started on the same day, were served by one pastor since they were combined as one charge; the pastor serving and preaching in the three different churches by turn.

From 1654-1676 the greatly loved Rev. Johannes Theodorus Polhemus was the Domine.

Compiled by Mrs. Kenn-Styker Rodda
of The Long Island Historical Society, Brooklyn

Episcopal

The American Episcopal Church is the autonomous expression in the United States of the world-wide Anglican communion. It is not the outgrowth of the Church of England in the colonies as much as it is a continuation of that church under a new constitution that makes the American branch independent of the mother church as the colonies became independent of the colonial empire.

The Episcopal Church first came to Long Island, as to all the colonies, as the Church of England; and until the Revolutionary War was under the jurisdiction of the Bishop of London. After the Revolutionary War the Church of England on Long Island, and elsewhere in the new nation, while having no intention of departing from the doctrine, discipline and worship of Canterbury and York, nevertheless, like the victorious colonies in their political structure, set up an autonomous independent church organization that became known as "The Protestant Episcopal Church in the United States."

There is no doubt that there were Church of England people on Long Island from the very earliest days of colonization, but organized parish groups with a resident priest did not appear until the early seventeen hundreds. It is recorded in William Manross' "History of the American Episcopal Church" that a Church of England missionary touring the colonies in 1702 reported

"in the colony of New York there were no Church ministers except in New York town."

Impetus to the establishment and growth of the church was provided by the English missionary society that received this report. The society, organized in 1701 and chartered by William III, was called "The Society for the Propagation of the Gospel in Foreign Parts," familiarly referred to as the "S.P.G." The importance of the work of the Society is best recognized in the realization that "nearly all ministers in these provinces were dependent in some measure upon the assistance of the Society, and the great majority would not have been able to continue their work at all without its help." The clergy on Long Island were no exception.

In 1693 an Act of Establishment of the Colonial Assembly of New York decreed that a "sufficient Protestant minister" should within a year be settled in the County of New York ... and two more in Queens County on Long Island. No provision was made for Kings County (Brooklyn), which was predominately Dutch, nor for Suffolk County, where the people were nearly all Independents.

"Sufficient Protestant minister" in English legal usage means a minister of the Established Church of England, but the Colonial New York Assembly was controlled by Dutch and dissenter members who, it appears, hoped that the term would not be interpreted to mean "any orthodox minister."

In Jamaica in particular, where one of the ministers under the act was to be located, this led to a running battle between the majority dissenting population and the colonial governor. After much pulling and tugging from 1702 the situation was finally stabilized in 1723 when the Episco- 19

Caroline Episcopal, Setauket
Chalice, paten and basin, 18th c.

palians succeeded in building a church of their own. This brought to a conclusion various suits to establish the right to a church building begun by the dissenters several years before and which the Established Church sought to take over in accord with the Act of 1693.

In Hempstead, where the other minister was to be established in accord with the Act of 1693, the situation was peaceful and quiet. From the first residency in 1704 of a Church of England minister to the present day the progress has been steady and peaceful. This atmosphere became true also in Jamaica after 1723. There have been internecene conflicts aplenty since that time but between dissenters and establishment there have been few occurrences of conflict in subsequent history.

The first establishment of the church in Suffolk County took place in Setauket, where a group of local citizens petitioned the S.P.G. to send a missionary to Brookhaven. In response to this request the S.P.G. in 1723 sent the Reverend James Wetmore, one of the group of so-called "Yale Converts." Under Mr. Wetmore and his successors the mission blossomed into Caroline Church of Brookhaven, which today is not only one of Long Island's cherished historic shrines but also a flourishing suburban parish.

The S.P.G. was responsible for the establishment of five centers on Long Island: Grace Church, Jamaica; St. George's, Flushing; St. George's, Hempstead; St. James, Elmhurst; and Caroline, Setauket. From these centers the church spread until now there are Episcopal Churches throughout the length and breadth of the Island.

The characteristic structure of the Episcopal Church requires the designation of a certain geographical area as a "diocese," which is placed under the jurisdiction of a bishop. This is so essential to the nature of the Episcopal Church that no history - no matter how short - can fail to make some mention of it.

All of Long Island is now a diocese and is known as the Diocese of Long Island under the jurisdiction of the Right Reverend James P. DeWolfe, the present bishop. But Long Island has not always been a separate diocese. For many years, in fact until after the Revolutionary War, it was part of the Diocese of London. After the Revolutionary War, and after the consecration of the first bishop of New York, Long Island was part of the Diocese of New York. It remained a part of New York until 1868, when it was organized as a diocese in itself; and from that date to this it has had four diocesans: the Right Reverend Abram Newkirk Littlejohn, the Right Reverend Frederick Burgess, the Right Reverend Ernest Milmore Stires, and the present Bishop, James P. DeWolfe.

Here is the essence of the history of the Episcopal Church on Long Island. Naturally much of great importance has been left unmentioned; but this effort will not have been in vain if but a small insight has been given into the Episcopal Church on Long Island, and great will be its worth if a piqued curiosity can only be assuaged by a longer and harder look.

John Priestley Mitton, Rector
Caroline Church of Brookhaven, Setauket

St. Mary's Episcopal, Ronkonkoma

Jewish

Although New York City is the site of the oldest Jewish Congregation in North America, dating from Dutch colonial days; and despite the fact that New York became the main center of Jewish life and worship after the American Revolution, there were no Jewish communities on nearby Long Island until well into the nineteenth century.

To be sure, individual Jews came to Long Island quite early. Asser Van Swellem Levy, who arrived in New Amsterdam with the pioneers of 1654, had his summer home in what is now Long Island City. Aaron Isaacs, grandfather of John Howard Payne, settled in Easthampton before 1750. Joshua Montefiore, uncle of the famed Sir Moses Montefiore, practiced law in Sag Harbor in the 1820's. Indeed

> "the whole Island was familiar country to New York Colonial Jewry ... In the 1760's there were Jewish settlers in South Haven, Easthampton and Jamaica" (Marcus: "Early American Jewry)
> But no synagogue.

The first Jewish congregation in all of Long Island was Congregation Beth Elohim (House of God) founded in Brooklyn in 1851. But the first synagogue building was that of Congregation Beth Israel, dedicated in 1862. It had been purchased from the Calvary Protestant Episcopal Church.

In what is today called "The Island," the oldest synagogues are not in the counties of Queens or Nassau, but in Suffolk. No doubt it was the greater distance from New York City that made it impracticable for these country folk to travel to town for religious communion. More likely, the coming of the railroad, the consequent growth of some light industry, and the resulting influx of population in post-civil-war times provided the stimulus.

It was in 1870 that Thomas Welwood and Charles Schleier founded the "City" of Breslau, now Lindenhurst, on the south shore. This was Long Island's first real-estate boom. Four and a half years later, a committee of citizens in the new settlement incorporated the Jewish congregation Neta Szarschea. But apparently the community did not grow. No synagogue was built. Not until 1913 was a fresh start made, when the Hebrew Congregation of Lindenhurst was again incorporated. Its synagogue, dedicated in 1915, was replaced by the present structure in the 1930's.

The fact is that growing communities are likely to replace their original houses of worship to meet increasing needs. This is what happened in Brooklyn, where none of the nineteenth century synagogues is in use. As a result, the oldest existing synagogues on Long Island, even if we include Brooklyn, are two modest white wooden sanctuaries in Suffolk County - one in East Setauket, the other in Sag Harbor. Both owe their birth to the influx of Jewish industrial workers in the 70's and 80's. Both declined with the decline of the industries involved. And both synagogues were revived in the great new surge of growth on Long Island that followed the Second World War.

In East Setauket the Congregation Agudath Achim (Band of Brothers), now known as the North Shore Jewish Center, was incorporated in 1893. It is clear that the community had been meeting for worship in private homes for some years before that date - even before 1870, when the J.W. El-

23

berson rubber factory was opened in the village, giving employment to a number of Jewish immigrants. The synagogue itself appears to have been built just before the turn of the century.

In Sag Harbor there stands Temple Adas Israel (Congregation of Israel), built in 1899-1900. Here, too, the small group of Jewish pioneers was augmented after 1870 by newcomers who came to work in a factory - in this case, the Fahys Watch Case Company. Here, too, worship had been conducted in private homes for at least a decade before the synagogue was built.

Another little synagogue stands in Greenport, where a congregation was formed in 1902, long after Nathan Kaplan had pioneered out there in the 1860's. Kaplan Avenue bears his name.

From these small beginnings, Long Island Jewry has grown, its growth paralleling the population explosions of the Island itself, particularly in the 20's and the 50's.

Before the First World War, Suffolk had added congregations in Bay Shore, Bellport, Patchogue, Huntington and Riverhead. In Queens and Nassau, the earliest synagogues were in Glen Cove, Hempstead, Jamaica, Richmond Hill and the Rockaways.

But the real leap forward came after 1920, and again in the post-war years 1945-55. Some very large congregations have grown up in the past three decades - in places like Forest Hills, Kew Gardens, Flushing, Great Neck, Rockville Centre and so on. Today a traveller can stop for Jewish worship at almost every town from Bay Ridge to Sag Harbor. A very recent addition is the Jewish Center of the Hamptons, on Montauk Highway in Easthampton.

Some of these congregations - Orthodox, Conservative or Reform - worship in magnificent edifices of modern architectural design, adorned with Holy Arks, Torah curtains, menorahs and other religious symbols created by leading contemporary craftsmen. Others continue to be at home in the simpler sanctuaries of earlier days. All, it is to be hoped, strive to add something of lasting worth to the spiritual fibre of Long Island's citizenry.

Rabbi S. Gershon Levi
Jamaica Jewish Center

Lutheran

Algemeen Rijksarchief petition, 1653, The Hague, reads:

"... from the Lutherans in New Netherlands to the States General
... Noble, High and Mighty Lords, the States General of the United
Netherlands ... we, residing under the jurisdiction of New Netherlands on the Manhattans at Fort Orange, as well as on Long Island
petition that your High Mightiness will ... kindly consent that the
doctrine of the Augsburg Confession may be ... publicly taught and
practiced here in this country and that a pastor of the said faith,
maintained at our own expense, may be tolerated".

Today, there are 211 Lutheran churches
with 151,470 members on Long Island, but for two hundred years after 1653 Long Island
Lutherans had to ferry to churches in Manhattan. Between 1841 and 1847 three congregations in Brooklyn were formed and still exist today at practically the original lo-
cations. Two of these have been members of Lutheran synods since 1847 - St. John's
the Evangelist, on Maujer Street, and St. John's on New Jersey Avenue.

Transportation was a prime factor in
church mission activity. The completion of the Long Island Railroad from Brooklyn to
Hicksville brought Lutheran activity into what is now Nassau County earlier than it
appeared in the present Queens County. In 1850 Trinity Lutheran was organized. In
Hicksville a large portion of the settlers were Dutch and German and of the Lutheran
faith. Circuit rider pastors from Brooklyn served the congregation for the first 14
years. Today, this congregation worships in a large compound of buildings on West
Nicholai Street directly across from where the small school house stood which served
as their first place of worship.

Two congregations can lay claim to be-
ing the first Lutheran church in Queens. Such honorable distinctions are difficult
to define because of insufficient or lost records. St. John's in College Point was
begun as a mission in 1853 and organized as a congregation in 1857. The early records
of Trinity Lutheran Church in Middle Village were lost in a fire; 1863 is given as the
date of their formal organization, but there are evidences of the beginnings of this
congregation in the early 1850's when the Chapel in Lutheran Cemetery was the place of
worship.

The Long Island Railroad again served
the Lutherans as well as all other denominations in the churches' mission endeavors
when it completed the road to Suffolk County. The coming of the railroad made the
Greenport area boom between 1844 and 1848. In the early 1850's German and Polish
merchants and farmers were attracted there in considerable numbers. There were also
Lutheran whalers from the West Indies. In 1857 the beginnings of St. Peter's Lutheran Church appeared, and in 1866 the congregation was formally organized. Throughout
these years, St. Peter's Church has ministered to people working on the land and on
the sea and each Sunday in the early hours, there has been a service for fishermen.
In November of this year, the new church edifice of St. Peter's was dedicated.

In the forty years between 1841 and
1881, 22 of the present existing churches were organized, only 3 of which were in
Nassau-Suffolk. The completion of the Brooklyn Bridge encouraged many immigrants in
Manhattan to spread out into the more spacious areas. During the next forty years,

79 of the present congregations appeared on Long Island, 17 of them in Nassau-Suffolk.

In the recent forty years, more than half of the 110 now existing were organized in these two counties. Many nationality backgrounds are represented in these congregations - pre-Colonial American, German, Swedish, Norwegian, Danish, Finnish, Polish, Latvian and Estonian.

Institutions of health, welfare and education have frequently accompanied the growth of Lutheran churches, particularly in urban areas. Therefore, it is not surprising that a Lutheran college was organized in Brooklyn in the latter part of the 19th century and functioned during the first five years in a Lutheran church building. Upsala College is now located in East Orange, New Jersey. Neither is it surprising that during the same era, there were organized a number of Lutheran hospitals, medical centers, homes for children and the aged, and churches specifically for European seamen in port. All of these still exist.

The Mill Neck Manor, Lutheran School for the Deaf, is widely recognized within medical circles as a school for deaf and severely hard of hearing children who have mental ability to profit by school attendance. At present, 90 children are enrolled. There is also a service known as the Lutheran Friends of the Deaf, which offers spiritual care, counselling, job placement and does ear research.

Although Lutheran people were on Long Island from the very beginning, church buildings came late -- only a little over 100 years ago. But since then, mission activity has made Lutherans a leading denomination with more than half of its Long Island membership in Nassau-Suffolk.

Helen M. Knubel, Secretary, Research and Statistics
National Lutheran Council

Mannetto Hill, Methodist, erected 1855

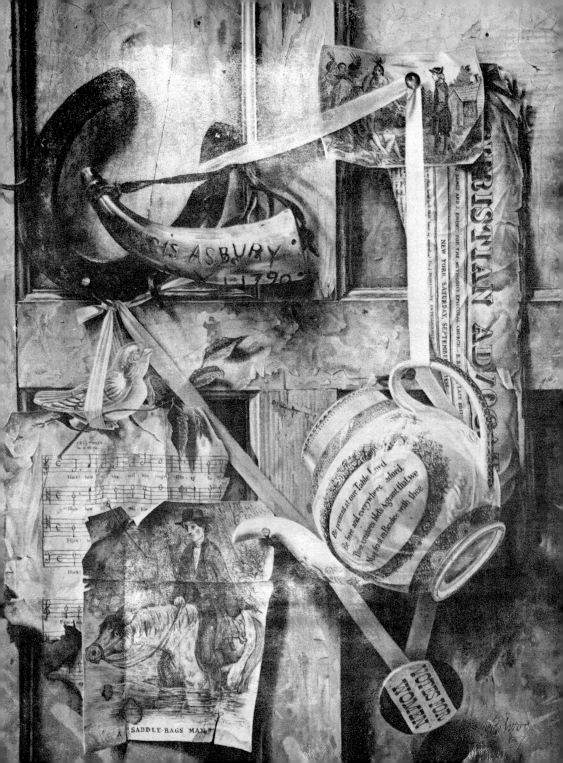

Methodist

The Methodist Church is a Church of Christ in which "the pure Word of God is preached, and the Sacraments duly administered." This Church is a great Protestant body, though it did not come directly out of the Reformation but had its origin within the Church of England. Its founder was John Wesley, a clergyman of that Church.

The Methodist Movement began to find adherents in England and soon spread to the Northern part of Ireland. In 1766 Philip Embury, a Methodist lay preacher from Ireland, came to America and began to preach in New York City. The Movement spread along the Atlantic Sea Coast and Westward, and on December 24, 1784 in Baltimore, some sixty lay preachers with Dr. Thomas Coke and Francis Asbury organized the Methodist Episcopal Church in America.

Captain Thomas Webb, a Methodist lay preacher and officer in the British Army, established Methodist preaching on Long Island at the home of James Harper in Newton (presently Middle Village in Queens), late in 1767. He organized a "class" appointing Harper as "leader," and the work was related to Philip Embury's original New York Society (presently the John Street Church.) James Harper gave property to the Newton group for their first chapel. (This James Harper was the grandfather of the four Harper brothers - James, John, Fletcher and Wesley, who founded the notable publishing house which still bears their names.)

Francis Asbury, one of the two first Bishops of American Methodism, visited Long Island at least nine times, and in his Journal, May 27, 1787, mentions the Harper's by name. Asbury made two brief preaching tours east of Newton, touching Hempstead, Hempstead Harbor (presently Roslyn) and Mosquito Cove (presently Glen Cove). These three settlements became centers of Methodist interest.

At Glen Cove, May 18-20, 1805, the first Methodist Camp Meeting on Long Island was conducted. It was led by Circuit Elder, William Thacher, and Asbury attended, preaching several times. "There were great crowds and conversions."

Other early Methodist points on Long Island were: From the records available, one of the oldest Methodist Societies on Long Island was that founded in Commack in 1783. The oldest Methodist Church building is the Commack Church, which was built in 1789.

In 1791 Ezra Tuttle of Blue Point, a rough sea-faring man of New England stock, was converted by a circuit rider, one Benjamin Abbott; and then got together a small group of neighbors and friends from Patchogue to found the Methodist Church there.

The Methodist Church of Amityville had its first meeting in 1792 in the home of Elijah Chichester.

The oldest church on the North Fork of Long Island is the Southold Methodist Church. Its first class meeting was held in June of 1794 and it became organized as a Methodist Society in 1795.

The Hauppage Methodist Church was organized as a Methodist Body in the year 1806. Soon after this, following the conversion of Mrs. Deborah Davis, Francis Ward and Henry Redstone, preachers in the Long Island Circuit were invited to come to Stony Brook. In 1809 a preaching appointment

31

was established and a class was formed in the home of Mrs. Davis, which is just four houses east of the present Suffolk Museum in Stony Brook.

Other early Methodist points on Long Island also included Port Jefferson, with a first Methodist Society in 1824, and Greenport, which became organized in 1828.

Long Island Methodism is presently divided into two districts which run its entire length. Within these districts there are one hundred and forty one Methodist churches with a total membership of sixty-nine thousand persons. In addition to our houses of worship we have within our area the first and one of the finest of Methodist hospitals - the Methodist Hospital of Brooklyn. The Bethany Deaconess Hospital is also one of our fine institutions.

Two homes for the aged serve this area, The Bethany Home and The Brooklyn Methodist Episcopal Church Home. The Methodist Church is presently seeking a site for a new home to be placed in either Suffolk or Nassau County. Camp Quinipet on Shelter Island is one of our Conference Youth Centers which is used all year but which provides a specialized institute-type program for our youth in the summer.

Methodism is, historically speaking, relatively new to Long Island. It takes its place alongside the other churches as it ministers to the changing scene which is Long Island. It rejoices in the fact that it is a part of the one Church of our Lord and shares in a common task. Its ecumenical spirit is still best expressed in John Wesley's words: "I desire to have a league, offensive and defensive, with every soldier of Christ. We have not only one faith, one hope, and one Lord, but are directly engaged in one warfare."

David C. Houston, The Setauket Methodist Church
and Richard J. Rice, The Community Church, Stony Brook

Landing Methodist Church, erected 1834

Presbyterian, Smithtown Branch

Presbyterian

Presbyterianism in the United States had its birth on Long Island where the oldest congregations are found. In 1640 a congregation from Lynn, Mass. settled in Southampton and one from New Haven came to Southold. "The first" title remains unsettled. Other congregations, still extant today, were soon to follow - Hempstead (1644), East Hampton (1650), Huntington (1658), Setauket (by 1660) and Jamaica (1662).

These first settlers found their attention drawn to the Indians who were here before them. Prior to 1658 William Leverich was at work among the Indians of Oyster Bay. The mission to the Shinnecocks, begun in 1660, exists as an independent church today and is the oldest Indian work still existing in this country. Samson Occum, a Mohegan, was sent to the Montauks in 1748 where he was ordained by the Presbytery of Suffolk in 1759. In modern times besides Shinnecocks and Poosepatucks work has been done among Iroquois steel workers in Brooklyn.

In colonial days Presbyterians represented a dissenting church which did not make for comfortable relations with the established Church of England. Under Gov. Cornbury at the turn of the century both Hempstead and Jamaica were dispossessed of their buildings in favor of S.P.G. missionaries. Jamaica did not regain its building until 1728.

Presbyterian history, in a very real sense, begins with the organization of the first presbytery in 1706 at Philadelphia. By 1716 the presbytery had grown to the point where it became a synod divided into four presbyteries, among them the presbytery of Long Island. Its first meeting was held in 1717 when Pumroy of Newtown, McNish of Jamaica and Phillips of Setauket ordained Samuel Gelston at Southampton.

The Great Awakening was soon to sweep the colonies. Its effects struck deep in the Presbyterian Church. The Scotch-Irish ministers objected to the revival and soon fell out with the New England men who favored it. The result was the schism of 1743 in which the Long Island churches cast their lot with the revival, although some of our churches were far from unanimous in this regard as papers in the Suffolk Museum's files indicate. In 1758 the schism was healed.

The American Revolution was hard on the Presbyterian churches of Long Island. Presbyterian ministers so favored the Revolutionary cause that Charles Inglis, Rector of Trinity, wrote in 1776 that he knew of no Presbyterian ministers "who did not, by preaching and every effort in their power, promote all the measures of the Congress, however extravagant." With the Island occupied by the British, Presbyterian churches were desecrated and the town of Huntington was devastated because of its Presbyterian pastor, "the old rebel," Ebenezer Prime. From 1775 until 1784 the Presbytery of Suffolk was unable to meet. On resuming meetings they recorded

> "The Presbytery by reason of the calamity of a Civil War, the Island being under the controls of the enimy, have been prevented meeting for a long time."

After the Revolution things improved. The Synod was expanded to the General Assembly in 1789. Prior to this momentous step the Presbytery of Suffolk asked to withdraw from its adherence to the Synod perhaps demonstrating a certain Congregational tendency which has long plagued Long Island churches. Fortunately they were persuaded to retain their ecclesiastical connection.

The early 1800's saw revivalism once again coming to the fore under leaders such as Lyman Beecher in East Hampton. The Old School was Scotch-Irish, anti-revival, strict confessionalist and pro-slavery. The New School was New England Puritan, pro-revival, liberal interpretation of the Confession and anti-slavery. Largely due to a national reaction to the Civil War, Long Island divided into two presbyteries. This schism was healed in 1870.

One might say that Presbyterianism on Long Island reached its heyday about the turn of the present century when the largest Presbyterian churches in the country were to be found in Brooklyn. It is indicative of present trends that the largest Presbyterian church on the Island today is Siloam, a Negro church in Brooklyn and the second largest is Old First Church, Huntington.

Over the centuries the Island has been variously divided for purposes of ecclesiastical administration, having been everything from a part of a presbytery to an entire synod. For well over a hundred years the Presbytery of Long Island was composed of the easternmost towns beginning with the Town of Brookhaven.

On January 1,1963, by action of the General Assembly, the presbytery boundaries were redefined to include all of Nassau and Suffolk Counties thus making a strong presbytery of 60 churches and over 30,000 members, and leading to the confident expectation that the brightest chapters in the history of the Presbytery of Long Island are yet to be written.

Donald R. Broad
Setauket Presbyterian Church

36

Presbyterian, Setauket
Silver communion cup, Van Dyke, 17th c.

Chapel, Sisters of St. Dominick, Amityville, 19th c.

OUR CHOICE
AL SMITH for PRESIDENT

Holy Father Blesses Archdiocese

Rome to attend the solemn can-
onization ceremonies of Blessed
Frances Xavier Cabrini on July
7 when she will become the first
U. S. citizen saint. The occa-

Roman Catholic

Probably we shall never know if Long Island was visited by St. Brendan or other Irish seafarers between the 6th and 9th centuries or if their Catholic co-religionists, the Vikings, began sailing to its neighborhood shortly later than the year 1000. Some historians have made such statements. An early explorer, Estevan Gomez, named Long Island the Island of the Apostles, on June 29, 1525.

Under the 17th Century Dutch Governor Peter Stuyvesant, the Jews, Lutherans and Quakers were tolerated. Very few Catholics came into the colony.

Sir Thomas Dongan, the Catholic Governor, entered Long Island in 1683. Following his departure the Catholic Faith grew slowly. Some of the early Acadians settled on Long Island.

In M. Burk's Sag Harbor home, in 1830, services were held for fifteen Irish and one Portuguese family. On his rare trips to New York, he pleaded for a priest from St. James; in 1832 Father Patrick Moran arrived - the third Catholic Church was established on Long Island!

In 1838 St. Monica's in Jamaica was founded. In 1840 Mass was celebrated in Huntington and North Hempstead and Oyster Bay. In 1841 it was celebrated in Smithtown and in 1844 in Riverhead. By 1850 Southold and Greenport had active parishes, also Babylon and Patchogue.

Pope Pius IX elected Long Island into the Diocese of Brooklyn. In 1888 the Setauket Church was formed. In 1895 there were parishes in Freeport, Mineola, Valley Stream, Lynbrook, Baldwin, Floral Park, Seaford, all in Nassau and in Suffolk, Brentwood, Kings Park, Huntington, St. James, Blue Point, Cutchogue, Wading River, Southampton, Manorville.

It is interesting to note that Elizabeth Bayley Seton, a Protestant converted to the Catholic religion, became the foundress of the American Sisters of Charity. She is known to have spent parts of the summers of 1796, 1798 and 1803 on Long Island with her children. She has now been canonized by the Church as one of the first American saints.

Pope Pius XII divided the Diocese of Brooklyn into half and the new half became the Diocese of Rockville Centre, which now is the largest diocese in the United States and has almost 1,000,000 Catholics within its borders.

Father Arthur Herold, Pastor
St. James Church, Setauket

39

Sketch of First Unitarian Church, Brooklyn Heights, 1844
Architect Minard Lefever

Unitarian

The Unitarians and Universalists were two separate Protestant denominations until the spring of 1960, when they merged to form a Unitarian Universalist Association. It was a natural merger, for both were small denominations with similar and frequently overlapping histories, and both had similar liberal religious traditions.

On Long Island, the Association brings together eight churches and six Fellowships including the most recently formed Unitarian Fellowship of The Three Villages. All of these Fellowships and four of the churches have been established since 1944.

Two-thirds of the total membership on Long Island has been Unitarian or Universalist for less than seven years, and so a full history of the movement is largely a recent one. Its origins, however, are contained in the histories of only two churches established in the 1830's, the First Unitarian Congregationalist Society of Brooklyn, and the First Universalist Church of Southold, which were the sole representatives of both denominations on Long Island until 1905.

The first Unitarian society was organized in Brooklyn in 1833, and was strong enough by 1835 to acquire a small building and incorporate under the name of The First Unitarian Society of Brooklyn. It was composed largely of families recently come from New England who had brought with them a Unitarian theology strongly mixed with Congregationalist ideas of church government. Legend says that the newly formed Society issued a call to Ralph Waldo Emerson, who had just resigned as a minister to The Second Church of Boston. No doubt Emerson was considered as a candidate, but the call went instead to a Rev. David Barlow in 1834.

Internal theological differences split the Society for a brief time, leading to a reorganization and establishment in 1842 of the presently constituted First Unitarian Congregationalist Society of Brooklyn. At the same time it was a "Declaration of Faith" which contained the important proviso that it was "not to be considered as a pre-requisite to admission in this church." Although the Declaration may appear conservative in the light of present standards, and although the proviso was no doubt born of organizational necessity, it contained the liberal Unitarian thought of the time, including the idea of doctrinal tolerance which has become so characteristic of modern Unitarian-Universalism.

Two years later the Society dedicated its church, called "The Church of the Savior" which stands today at Pierrepont Street and Monroe Place. It is of size and elegance that seem unreasonably lavish for the small congregation of that day. But the building is now a matter of particular pride of the Brooklyn congregation, because it was designed by Minard Lefever, a prominent American architect of the period and it is considered an outstanding example of the Gothic revival. The church has been designated a historic landmark by the City of New York. Some of Mr. Lefever's original sketches are preserved in the Church archives.

Brooklyn soon became large enough for a Second and Third Unitarian Society, organized in 1851 and 1868. The first pastor of the Second Society was Samuel Longfellow, younger brother of Henry Wadsworth Longfellow, who was also a liberal religious trailblazer of sorts. He preached abolition too early to be popular, making it difficult to collect pew rentals. As one man of the parish recalled, "some of us went around and let all the benches, and then Mr.

Longfellow preached a John Brown sermon and drove them all away."

Longfellow's successors seem to have followed his trailblazing example in different ways, for although all three Brooklyn societies pioneered much of the 19th century urban social work, the Second Society also established a prominent record in philosophical inquiry.

The Brooklyn Ethical Association which grew out of a series of Sunday meetings developed into a forum for lecturers such as Samuel Gompers or historian John Fiske. By 1888 the list of corresponding members included several Hindu and other Oriental liberals, Herbert Spencer in England and Andrew White in Ithaca. White quoted Tolstoi as considering the publications of the Association among the best things that had come to him from America.

The Second and Third Societies did not stay long separated from the parent church, however, and in the mid-1920's they merged again with the First Church to comprise the present Unitarian congregation in Brooklyn.

Far less information is available concerning the equally long and distinguished history of the First Universalist Church at Southold. We know, however, that it was organized in 1835, and very soon acquired a house of modest dimensions (35 x 48 ft); and that on October 17 of that year a constitution, remarkable for its simplicity and liberalism, was filed with the Town Clerk. These appear to have been years of unusual religious discussion and ferment, with countless pamphlets, lectures and periodicals, as well as sermons all arguing weighty questions of salvation and creed.

The early history of the Universalist denomination in this country was furthermore considered very controversial, with strong feelings for and against it. In this context, the broad religious tolerance of the Southold trustees is impressive, for absolutely no creedal test was imposed on members of the congregation. Only the trustees must

"openly acknowledge the Universality of the Grace of God and avow their belief in the final holiness of all mankind."

This is a Christian code which is as surprising for what it does not contain, as for what it does. In addition, provision was made that any denomination of Christians might worship in the Church whenever it was not needed by Universalists.

Although it is not specifically documented, it may be supposed that the Southold Church stayed abreast of other Universalist churches theologically during the years that followed. The denomination as a whole became largely Unitarian in the 19th century, moving away from the Calvinism of its American founder, Rev. John Murray (1720-78). This was surely a significant turning in the history of the Universalist Church, for among other things it made possible the recent merger between the Unitarian and Universalist denominations.

In the first forty years of this century, two new Unitarian churches appeared on Long Island, the First Unitarian Church of Flushing, organized in 1905, and the Hollis Unitarian Church in 1924. These were lean years financially, and the two churches reported chronic debt during their early periods, which strained the resources of the two small congregations. In fact, the American Unitarian Association voted in April, 1924, to discontinue its effort to establish the Hollis church; but the congregation was determined to maintain its small outpost of liberal religion and only intensified its fund-raising efforts. Their

42

fight was successful and in November, 1924, the AUA reversed its decision giving Hollis Society support and recognition.

It was the Flushing Church which sponsored the Hollis Society through the efforts of their minister, Dr. Edwin Fairley, whose own salary was in frequent doubt. Once established, the two Societies worked together very closely and developed the Long Island leadership which, following the example of Dr. Fairley, was to pay off in the rapid expansion of Unitarianism after 1944.

The recent history of Unitarian-Universalism is distinguished for its expansion throughout Long Island. The first of the newest societies was formed in Plandome in 1944, and has been of invaluable assistance in helping the other societies which followed it in rapid succession. These include the Unitarian churches in Hempstead and Freeport, a Unitarian Society at Bay Shore, and Fellowships at Bellport, Muttontown, Northport, Port Washington, The Three Villages, and Syosset.

It is clearly no longer possible to record the history of Unitarian-Universalism on Long Island in terms of a few selected church histories. What happens to organized liberal religion in this area will now depend as much on how these various societies interact with each other; and the significance and general import of this has yet to be determined.

Richard A. Mould, Historian
Unitarian Fellowship of The Three Villages

Quakers

(RELIGIOUS SOCIETY OF FRIENDS)

The history of the Society on Long Island is, in its earliest phases, the history of the growth of religious tolerance in America.

The first Quakers known to have landed on Long Island arrived in 1657 when a ship, enroute to Boston, was blown off course and put in at New Amsterdam. The five Quaker missionaries abroad (three men and two women) seized the opportunity to preach and thereby roused the stern, Dutch ire of Gov. Peter Stuyvesant.

Four of the Quakers were forthwith shipped back to Boston and the leader, one Robert Hodgson, was imprisoned for over a year and flogged till, we are told, only the pleas of the Governor's sister saved his life.

The Dutch government of New Amsterdam remained inhospitable to "such dissident sects as Quakers" as one proclamation calls them. However, Quakers continued to enter the colony, to preach there, and to convert the inhabitants, most of whom appear to have been more tolerant than the Governor. It was in 1657, the very year the first Quakers landed, that the citizens of Flushing addressed to Peter Stuyvesant the now famous Flushing Remonstrance in which they took him to task for forbidding the harboring or entertaining of Quakers. One of the proudest entries in the record of religious tolerance is the statement of these sturdy burghers that, "if any of these said persons come in love unto us, we cannot in conscience lay violent hands upon them, but give them free egresse and regress unto our town, and houses, as God shall persuade our consciences."

Persecution continued, however, and Quakers continued for some time to be equated with witches and similar abominations. In 1660 one Mary Wright of Oyster Bay achieved the distinction of being the only woman on Long Island ever accused of witchcraft. She was, however, removed for trial to Massachusetts where it was felt that these things were better understood. When the charge of witchcraft failed, poor Mary was found guilty of "quakerism, a crime of equal enormity" according to the court, and was sentenced to banishment.

In 1662, John Bowne of Flushing was arrested and fined for allowing Quakers to worship in his house and refused to promise to desist. When he was arrested a second time, he was fined again and expelled from the colony. Instead of disappearing like so many others before him, Bowne made his way to Holland where he presented his case before the Dutch West India Company and was permitted to return to New Amsterdam after an absence of two years.

While the persecutions continued, Shelter Island, between Long Island's eastern forks, shared with Rhode Island the reputation of being the only safe refuge for a Quaker. Though its name was actually derived from the Indians, this island under the leadership of its freeholder, Nathaniel Sylvester, sheltered many a Quaker refugee from the intolerance of Dutch and of Puritan alike.

The transfer of the government to the English in 1664 eased the persecution but didn't solve all the problems of Quakers who wanted to practice their principles and still take their places in the world they lived in. In 1691, for example, John Bowne and Nathaniel Pearsall were elected to the General Assembly but refused on religious grounds to "swear the oath" and were dismissed and new elections ordered.

Gradually, however, Quakers began to play a larger role in the economy, and government of Long Island, and many of its communities. A Meeting House was built at Matinecock as early as 1671; one at Jericho in 1676; at Flushing in 1694, Bethpage in 1698, and Westbury in 1702. Quaker worship had become free by this time and the Society of Friends flourished.

As the Society grew it began producing men as notable for their preaching as their ancestors had been for stubborn resistance to persecution. Prominent among these was Elias Hicks who was born in Hempstead in 1748 and worked his Long Island farm between preaching tours. He was an ardent anti-slavery worker and when, in 1827, a division occurred in the Society of Friends, he was the leader of the liberal group who became known as Hicksites while the more conservative Quakers were called Orthodox. The town of Hicksville, founded after Elias Hicks' death, was named in his honor.

In the present century, Quakers on Long Island have survived a period of quietism and decline, have healed the ideological split of Hicks' day and - particularly since the Second World War - have flourished again. Active meetings (many in historic Meeting Houses) are to be found in Brooklyn, Flushing, Westbury, Matinecock, Manhasset, Jericho, Bethpage, Riverhead and St. James.

Thomas E. Tornquist
East Setauket

46

Eastern Orthodox

There are 1,500,000 Greek Orthodox Christians in America. They are scattered in every state of the Union and are citizens of the remotest villages. Their greatest concentration, however, is in the 10 largest cities of the United States.

Before the turn of the century, there were scarcely a few thousand Greeks in America; however, after 1900 the stream of immigrants built up after World War I.

Wherever a few score gathered they immediately sensed a lack of common worship and conducted private drives to get their village Priest to come to America for a short time; then all would return to their homeland in a financial position to alleviate the common economic plight in Greece. As we know, the temporary condition soon became permanent, and the Greek Orthodox remained. They have become model citizens of our Great Country.

It was not until the beginning of the second decade of this Century that the Church was formally organized by the arrival of an Archbishop from Greece. Greek Orthodoxy was now an integrate part of the religious life of America. Even though the Greek Orthodox Church is the oldest root of Christianity, we might say that it is one of the youngest in America. The many beautiful edifices that adorn our cities in America are the result of the love of the Greek for his church. One great example is the Byzantine Church of St. Paul's on Cathedral Avenue in Hempstead. It is one of the most beautiful buildings in our area.

Greek Orthodoxy is comparatively new in America and thus to Long Island (Nassau and Suffolk). The writer of these few paragraphs initiated this history by organizing the first Greek Orthodox Church in Nassau and Suffolk Counties in September 1950. Prior to that time the Greek Orthodox as far east as Greeport and Montauk had to travel to Jamaica or Corona to attend church services and receive Communion at least on the High Holy Days.

Arriving from New York in 1950, knowing very little of the Island, I soon discovered that I was to become an expert explorer visiting and ministering to the Greek Orthodox of both Counties with Hempstead as the starting point. The faithful in both Counties numbered about 250 families. The first edifice was constructed on Greenwich Street in Hempstead with about 350 seats. The growth of Nassau and presently Suffolk is well known. The Greek Orthodox who poured over to Nassau were in proportion. St. Paul's on Greenwich was already getting rather tight after only 2 years of life. By 1952 a new group with the blessing of the Hempstead Church had organized in Blue Point and thus the second church was built on the Island.

By 1955 new property was purchased by St. Paul's on Cathedral Avenue. The old edifice was sold to the R. C. Church of Our Lady of Loretto and construction of the present edifice on Cathedral Avenue was under way by 1957 after almost 2 years of planning and fund-raising. The cost of the church and Parish Center exceeded $1,200,000 and serves the needs of 2,000 families in Nassau.

A new Parish came into being in Huntington in 1955; still another one in Port Jefferson in 1959; a year later the Greek Orthodox in Babylon organized a congregation and this made the fourth church in Suffolk with Hempstead the only one in Nassau. The second Greek Orthodox Church in Nassau saw its beginning in 1963 in Freeport.

There is no doubt that in the near future, other churches will sprout in the fast growing areas, and new buildings of the church of old will bring before many other people the most ancient traditions and expressions of the Christian undivided Church.

All Greek Orthodox Churches in the Americas are under the Greek Orthodox Archbishop of N. & S. America, Iakovos, whose See is in New York City. His superior is the Ecumenical Patriarch, His Holiness, Athenagoras I, who sits on the throne of the Great Doctor of the Church St. John the Chrysostom in Istanbul, and of course is a successor to St. Andrew the Apostle and first called to the Disciples.

The Greek Orthodox Church is Apostolic not only from St. Andrew but from the Greatest of all Christian Missionaries, St. Paul, who spent most of his time organizing churches in Asia Minor and Greece. The Church adheres to the dogmas as interpreted by the 7 Ecumenical Councils of the undivided Church, and believes in 7 Sacraments.

Father George Papadeas
Dean of the Archiocesan Cathedral

Acknowledgements

FRONTISPIECE

Folk art sculpture, HENRY WARD BEECHER, attributed to Corbin, an Indiana farmer. In the Abby Aldrich Rockefeller Folk Art Collection, Williamsburg, Virginia.

Henry Ward Beecher was installed, as pastor of the Brooklyn Plymouth Church (Congregational), in 1847.

GENESIS

We are grateful to Dr. David Corey for giving us permission to use parts of his manuscript for our introduction.

TOMBSTONE

Grave of Thomas Cornwell, private cemetery, Far Rockaway. Inscription reads:

> "To the memory of Thomas (Cornwell,Esq). His weeping
> (widow) erects this monument (of her) affection and
> his age. Born 28 July AD 1703, he died (the 24th of)
> March 1764. What he (was to the) poor and to the
> Publick (the last) of which (he) served 27 years (in
> the) General Assembly of New York is engraved on tab-
> lets (more) durable than this (stone)."

> Parentheses indicate missing parts of
> shattered heavy slate tombstone.

PHOTOGRAPHS

Photographs in this booklet courtesy of Harvey A. Weber, Centerport, without whose long interest these photographic views would have been, for ever, lost.

CHAPTER ILLUSTRATIONS
CHAPTER ILLUSTRATIONS

Aaron Bohrod's ecclesiastical representations have been loaned to the Suffolk Museum for the Exhibition, "Ecclesiastical Art of Long Island," by LOOK Magazine. Photographs of these paintings are also courtesy of LOOK Magazine.

AUTHORS

These monographs were prepared by ministers and interested laymen in our area; without their help and cooperation this project would not have been possible.

51

BAPTISTS   8

Symbols depicted in the painting include an early picture of John the
Baptist; pages from Burmese and Baptist bible translations and a 19th
century edition of Bunyan's "Pilgrim's Progress"; jug carried by Isaac
Backus, champion of religious liberty; spectacles of Benjamin Randall
and portraits of John Mason Peck, Roger Williams, Richard Furman and
Lott Carey, a pioneer Negro missionary.

CHRISTIAN SCIENTISTS   10

The painting includes a portrait of founder Mary Baker Eddy; her gold
and ivory pen and manuscript "Hymn of Science"; announcement of services
(1880's); gavel given to Mother Church in Boston by Mrs. Eddy; Rembrandt's
print depicting Christ healing the sick and a pink rose - Mrs. Eddy's fa-
vorite flower.

CONGREGATIONALISTS   12

From the faith of the Pilgrims Bohrod depicts a page from Eliot's 1661
Indian Bible, title page of the "Bay Psalm Book" - the first printed
in the colonies; the first American woodcut, picturing Richard Mather;
colonial hourglass used to mark the lengthy sermons of early preachers;
an ear of Indian corn and an artist's conception of the Mayflower.

EPISCOPALIANS   18

The first days of the English colonies are reflected in many of these
symbols: replica of chalice in Bruton Parish, Williamsburg; Bishop
Samuel Seabury's "Book of Common Prayer"; Baptism of Pocahontas by Rev.
Alexander Whitaker; Byzantine cross worn by the Bishop of New York; arms
of the See of Canterbury; emblem of the Protestant Episcopal Church.

JEWS   23

These symbols of freedom are easily identifiable: Torah carried during
World War II by flying chaplain Rabbi Gordon; Washington's letter to
congregation of Newport, R.I. pledging religious freedom; 18th century
ram's horn with inscription; Prayer shawl of Revolutionary War patriot
Gershom Mendes Seixas; silver kiddush cup made by Paul Revere and an
52 Israeli stamp honoring Albert Einstein.

Symbols represented are the fish, carved by an Alaskan Eskimo; Holy
Virgin mosaic from Sofia at Constantinople; priest's hand cross,1880,
by Ovchinnikov; sketch of cathedral in Sitka, Alaska, first Orthodox
diocese in New World (1848); part of Russian-Aleut Bible, translated
1828.

END PAGE

Indian Cemetery, Shinnecock Reservation, Southampton. Center grave shown is that of
the last 8 full-blooded Shinnecock who lost their lives in a rescue attempt.

Photo courtesy Harvey A. Weber, taken 1941

Notes

Notes

THE OMEGA. . .
AND
THE ALPHA. . .